God's Whispers

His Voice, Our Journey

Sharon Fernandes

BookLeaf Publishing

India | USA | UK

This book is dedicated to my family, whose love has been a living testament to God's grace in its purest form. Your unwavering encouragement to walk in His path has been my strength, and your steadfast faith in me has shaped my own. You have celebrated my acts of kindness, corrected me when I've faltered, and guided me toward growth and understanding.

This book is a reflection of your love, guidance, and the strong foundation you've given me to walk in God's light.

May He continue to bless each of you abundantly, as He has so graciously blessed me.

Acknowledgement

First and foremost, I give all glory and thanks to my Almighty God, Jehovah, and my Saviour, Jesus Christ, whose love is the foundation of my life. Their infinite grace has carried me through every challenge, teaching me to trust in Their plan and walk in faith. Through Their love, I have come to understand the true essence of peace, hope, and purpose, and I am forever grateful for Their guidance.

To my dear family and friends, the precious gifts God has blessed me with—support has been my pillar of strength in my life, and for that, I am deeply grateful.

Preface

"God's Whispers" is a personal journey of discovering the characters that God wants us to embody in our daily lives. This book outlines more than thirty essential traits that reflect God's heart, such as love, patience, humility, and kindness. Each character is defined with clarity, supported by Bible verses that illustrate God's word, and accompanied by practical examples to help you integrate these virtues into your everyday walk.

At the end of each reflection, take a moment to ask yourself, "Do I live this trait?" This is not about striving for perfection; it's about embracing the journey. With each entry, you will find new opportunities to grow, and with each moment of reflection, you'll draw closer to the heart of God's purpose for your life.

Let this book serve as both inspiration and a gentle reminder that God's whispers are not distant commands but loving invitations calling you to become the person, He has designed you to be.

Love

Jesus replied, "Love the Lord your God with all your heart and with all your soul and with all your mind". This is the first and greatest commandment.
Matthew 22:37,38

You are here today because of your love for God. We cannot offer Him anything; all we can do is honor Him by living in obedience to His commandments.
To love God is to seek His will, understand His desires, and faithfully follow His path. At the core of it , our purpose is clear: to bring glory to God through the way we live—through our choices, our actions, and show our love to Him and the people around us.

Love others as you love yourself

"Love your neighbour as yourself.'
Matthew 22:39

Loving others as we love ourselves means treating people with the same kindness and respect we'd want to receive. It's about understanding their feelings, just like we care about our own.

When Jesus said, "Love your neighbor as yourself", he wasn't just talking about the people we like. He meant everyone—our

friends, strangers, and even those who
challenge us.

Here are a few everyday examples:
· Help a friend in need without expecting
anything in return.
· Pray for your friends, family, and even those
who may have wronged you, asking God to
bless and guide them.

Rejoice

"Rejoice in the Lord always. I will say it again:
Rejoice!"
Philippians 4:4

To "rejoice" means to experience profound joy
and delight. It is not merely about feeling
happy because things are going well; it's about
finding joy in God, regardless of the
circumstances. This happens when you know
God is in control and knowing that he has
good plans for you.
It's a joy that resides within, anchored in your
relationship with Him, rather than what's
happening in the world around you.

Here are few everyday examples:
· Maintaining a positive outlook even in the face of adversity.
· Constantly thinking about all the good things that have happened and being happy.
· Singing worship songs or hymns and rejoicing in the Lord.

Faith

"Now faith is confidence in what we hope for
and assurance about what we do not see."
Hebrews 11:1

Faith is complete trust in God's promises. It is
the confidence to believe in something or
someone, even without tangible proof. Faith
means believing that everything happening
today is because of God's will, and finding
peace knowing that He is always with you.
It involves surrendering our fears and doubts,
trusting that He meets our needs and has a
perfect plan for our lives.

Here are few everyday examples:
· Praying with conviction, believing that God hears and answers.
· Trusting God's plan even in moments of uncertainty.
· Encouraging others to stay hopeful and trust in God's provision.

Contentment

"But godliness with contentment is great
gain."
1 Timothy 6:6

Contentment is a state of peaceful
satisfaction and acceptance, appreciating
what you have rather than constantly striving
for more. It is about focusing on the present
and valuing non-material aspects of life.
It is finding peace and satisfaction in God's
provision. It is about resting in his sufficiency,
regardless of circumstances.

Here are few everyday examples:
· Being content with basic needs like food
and clothing, as taught in 1 Timothy 6:8.
· Celebrate your achievements without envy
when others succeed.
· Avoid comparing yourself to others,
recognizing that your life and journey are
unique and filled with their own blessings.
· Enjoy the quiet moments, like a warm cup of
coffee or a peaceful walk, rather than always
chasing after something bigger or better.

Peace

"Blessed are the peacemakers, for they shall be called sons of God."
Matthew 5:9

Peace is more than just the absence of conflict; it's about wholeness, tranquility, and a deep sense of security rooted in your connection with God. This isn't based on circumstances but on the trust you have on God.

This peace empowers you to navigate stress, make wiser decisions, and remain content, regardless of life's challenges. It keeps you steady even when life feels chaotic. It's a gift from God that grows when you focus on him and his promises.

Here are a few everyday examples:
· Remaining calm during uncertainty.
· If a conversation is getting heated, choose to step back or respond calmly instead of escalating the situation.
· Using a calm and gentle tone of voice in stressful situations.

Patience

"Patience is better than pride."
Ecclesiastes 7:8

Patience is the ability to endure challenges, hardships or delays without losing faith or inner peace. It requires trusting in God's perfect timing. It is managing feelings of irritation or anger when things don't go as planned.

Here are a few everyday examples:
· Listening without interrupting and waiting your turn.
· Staying calm and patient during heavy traffic or delays, recognizing that getting upset doesn't change the situation.

· Being patient with children as they learn,
make mistakes, or ask repetitive questions,
understanding that growth takes time.

Kindness

"Be kind and compassionate to one another."
Ephesians 4:32

Kindness means choosing to help others, even when it's inconvenient. It could be as simple as offering a smile. It's a choice to put someone else's needs before your own and to show them love, just like God does for us. It's showing consideration and care for others. Being kind isn't always easy, especially when others may not extend the same courtesy to us. However, the Bible teaches us that kindness reflects God's love and helps build stronger, more meaningful relationships with those around us.

Here are a few everyday examples:
· Helping a stranger with directions.
· Tell someone they look nice, did a great job, or that you appreciate them.
· Assisting someone struggling to open a door, or cross the street without being asked.
· Using kind words like "please," "thank you," and "sorry," and show good manners in all interactions.

Faithfulness

"Let love and faithfulness never leave you;
bind them around your neck, write them on
the tablet of your heart."
Proverbs 3:3

Faithfulness means being devoted,
trustworthy, and unwavering, especially in
your relationship with God. It's about staying
committed to Him and His ways, no matter
what challenges or temptations come your
way.
It also means being dependable, standing firm
in righteousness even when it's hard. It's
about being someone people can count on

because your life reflects the same faithfulness
God shows us every day.

Here are a few everyday examples:
· Keeping your promises even when it's
difficult.
· Staying loyal to your family and friends by
being present during their times of need and
celebrating their joys.
· Working diligently and giving your best
effort at your place of work.

Prayer

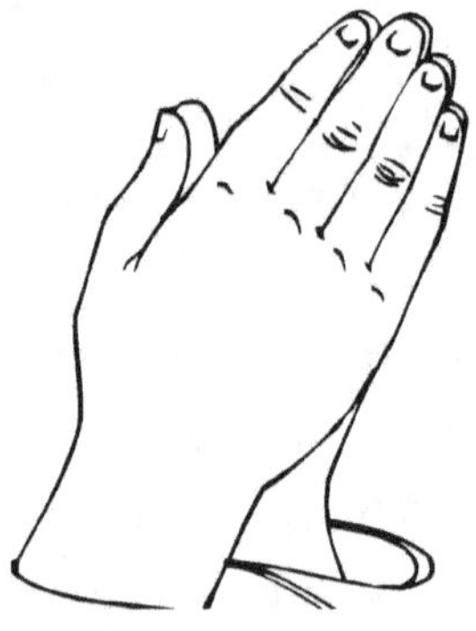

"Pray without ceasing."
1 Thessalonians 5:17

Prayer is a direct line to God, where we share our hearts, seek guidance, and align our will with His. It is pausing to communicate with God, whether in silence, spoken words, or even through a grateful heart.
Prayer can include praise, confession, thanksgiving, and supplication. It reflects our dependence on God. It is also about deepening our connection with Him.

Here are a few everyday examples:
· Start and end your day with a short prayer.
· Pray before making important decisions.
· Thank God for small blessings throughout
your day.

Self-Control

"Like a city whose walls are broken through is
a person who lacks self-control."
Proverbs 25:28

Self-control is the ability to manage your
emotions, actions, and desires, especially
when faced with challenges. It's about staying
disciplined and making choices that reflect
your values rather than giving in to impulsive
feelings or temptations.
It requires thinking long-term and choosing
what's best for you and others, rather than
succumbing to what feels easy or tempting in
the moment. It's not always easy, but with
practice and God's help, it becomes a part of
who you are.

Here are a few everyday examples:

- Resisting the urge to respond in anger during an argument.
- Not reacting to someone's rude comment on social media.
- Taking a deep breath and responding calmly when you're frustrated instead of yelling or lashing out.
- Turning down a bad habit or unhealthy influence, even if everyone else is doing it.

Humility

"Humble yourselves before the Lord, and he
will lift you up."
James 4:10

Humility means recognizing that you're not
above others and that everything you have -
your talents, successes, and blessings - comes
from God. It's about having confidence
without arrogance and treating everyone with
respect, no matter their situation.
It is about putting others first and remaining
grounded rather than being full of yourself.

Here are a few everyday examples:
· Sharing your successes without exaggerating or trying to make others feel less.
· Treating a janitor, cashier, or stranger with the same kindness and respect as you would a CEO.
· Acknowledging that your blessings, talents, or opportunities come from God, not just your own efforts.
· Recognizing your need for God's help in your decisions rather than relying only on yourself.

Compassion

"Be kind and compassionate to one another."
Ephesians 4:32

Compassion is about feeling deeply for
someone else's pain or struggles and being
moved to help them. It's not just sympathy;
it's about taking action to make things better.
Compassion reflects God's love for us, as He
is always ready to help in our time of
need. It's not about fixing everything but
showing care and making a difference, one act
at a time.
It's a key part of living a godly life-choosing
to care deeply for others and show love
through your actions.

Here are a few everyday examples:
· Visiting and comforting the sick or grieving.
· Spending time at a homeless shelter or
donating food to families in need.
· Speaking out against bullying or injustice
when you see someone being treated unfairly.
· Checking in on a lonely friend or offering to
help someone with their homework or chores.

Gratitude

"Give thanks in all circumstances; for this is God's will for you in Christ Jesus."
1 Thessalonians 5:18

Gratitude is about recognizing the blessings in your life and being thankful for them. It's not just about saying "thank you"; it's about having a heart that appreciates both the big and small gifts in life and acknowledging the hand of God in everything.
Practice gratitude not only when things are going great, but even during tough times, because it shows trust in God's plan and His goodness.
Gratitude shifts your mindset, helping you see life as a gift rather than a list of things you owe. It makes you more joyful, helps you

build stronger relationships, and keeps you grounded in God's love and provision.

Here are a few everyday examples:
· Thanking God daily for his blessings.
· Sending a text/email to your parents, friends, or mentors to let them know you're grateful for their support.
· Write down three things you are thankful for each day to focus on the positives in your life.
· Showing gratitude by appreciating your possessions, circumstances, and relationships without constantly seeking more.

Forgiveness

"Bear with each other and forgive one another
if any of you has a grievance against someone.
Forgive as the Lord forgave you."
Colossians 3:13

Forgiveness is the act of letting go of anger or
resentment toward someone. It does not
mean excusing harmful behavior or forgetting
the offense, but instead choosing not to let it
control your heart or actions.
It is releasing someone from the burden of
their wrongdoing. True forgiveness frees both
the forgiver and the forgiven from bitterness
and guilt. Forgiveness reflects God's love and
helps us move toward healing and
reconciliation.

Here are few everyday examples:
· Choosing to forgive a friend who has wronged you.
· Letting go of grudges against those who have wronged you, even if they haven't apologized.
· If a family member loses temper with you during the day, forgive quickly and remind yourself of how often God forgives us.
· Offer another opportunity to someone who failed or disappointed you.

Integrity

"Whoever walks in integrity walks securely,
but whoever takes crooked paths will be
found out."
Proverbs 10:9

Integrity is the quality of being honest and
having a strong character. It is doing what is
right even when no one is watching. It is
about living a life that reflects deep moral
conviction, fairness, consistency and
accountability in all areas of life.

Here are a few everyday examples:
· Returning extra change accidentally given to you by a cashier, even if no one else would know.
· Following through on commitments even when it's inconvenient.
· Standing firm in faith and refusing to compromise biblical values for worldly gain.
· Refusing to accept a bribe, even under pressure.
· Charging customers fairly and delivering the quality you promise.

Courage

"Be strong and courageous. Do not be afraid;
do not be discouraged, for the Lord your God
will be with you wherever you go."
Joshua 1:9

Courage is the ability to confront fear,
challenges, or danger while staying true to
your values and convictions. It means acting
with strength and confidence, even when
faced with fear, uncertainty, or opposition.
Being courageous doesn't mean being fearless
but rather choosing to act despite fear.
Courage can be physical, like risking personal
safety to help others, or moral, like defending
the truth and standing firm in your beliefs,
even when it's unpopular or difficult.

Here are a few everyday examples:
· Standing up for what's right even when it's hard.
· Speaking up for someone being mistreated.
· Ask for what you need or deserve, such as a raise, support, or clarity, even if it feels uncomfortable.

Hope

"But those who hope in the LORD will renew their strength. They will soar on wings like eagles; they will run and not grow weary, they will walk and not be faint."
Isaiah 40:31

Hope is a positive outlook that anticipates good outcomes and believes in possibilities. It is the confident expectation of God's promises and the eternal joy found in Him. It is the belief that good things are possible, even in difficult times.
It provides strength and motivation to persevere through difficulties, helping individuals stay optimistic about the future.

Here are a few everyday examples:
· Staying positive in tough situations because
of trust in God.
· Encouraging others to stay positive and
resilient.
· Staying focused on long-term aspirations,
even if progress seems slow, knowing that
persistence leads to growth and success.
· Continue to take small steps forward, even
after facing disappointments, with the hope
that each effort brings you closer to your goal.

Honesty

"The Lord detests lying lips, but he delights in
people who are trustworthy."
Proverbs 12:22

Honesty is the foundation of trust, requiring truthfulness, transparency, and trustworthy in all interactions. It is living in alignment with truth before God and others, reflecting His righteousness. Being honest involves telling the truth, even when it feels difficult or uncomfortable. It's about being authentic in your relationships, admitting mistakes, and expressing genuine thoughts and intentions without deceit.

Honesty strengthens trust, nurtures meaningful relationships, and reflects a person's commitment to doing what is right.

Here are a few everyday examples:
· Not hiding mistakes but admitting them.
· Being transparent in work or business dealings.
· Giving back something you find that doesn't belong to you, such as a wallet or a misplaced phone.
· Abiding workplace policies, or community rules, even when no one is watching.

Generosity

"Each of you should give what you have
decided in your heart to give, not reluctantly
or under compulsion, for God loves a cheerful
giver."
2 Corinthians 9:7

Generosity is the act of giving freely and
wholeheartedly, expecting nothing in
return. It is selflessly offering your time,
resources, and love to others as an expression
of God's love. True generosity stems from a
heart of compassion, rooted in the desire to
uplift and support those in need.

Here are a few everyday examples:
· Donating to those in need or supporting a charitable cause.
· Offering your time to help a friend or volunteer.
· Sharing your knowledge or skills to uplift others.

Submission

"Submit yourselves to God. Resist the devil,
and he will flee from you."
James 4:7

Submission is the willingness to accept guidance and authority with humility and cooperation. It is yielding to God's authority and trusting His plans, as well as respecting those He places in leadership.
It involves setting aside personal desires or preferences to honor and follow God by aligning one's heart and actions with God's will, trusting his wisdom and plan above one's own. It is not about weakness but about strength in choosing "Submission".

Here are a few everyday examples:

· Surrendering your plans to God's will through prayer and obedience.

· Respecting the decisions of a leader or authority figure, even if you disagree.

· Being open to feedback and acting on it constructively.

Hospitality

"Do not forget to show hospitality to strangers, for by so doing some people have shown hospitality to angels without knowing it."
Hebrews 13:2

Hospitality is an act of welcoming others, especially strangers, with kindness and openness, showing God's love through actions. It's inviting people into your home or life with warmth and generosity. It's about serving others selflessly, not out of obligation but as a reflection of God's love and grace. Spiritual hospitality sees every guest as a gift

and every opportunity to serve as a way to
honor God.

Here are a few everyday examples:
- Invite someone to share a meal or coffee,
especially someone who might be lonely.
-Greeting new colleagues warmly and helping
them feel included in the workplace.
=Smile and greet others, making them feel
welcomed and valued.

Zeal

"Never be lacking in zeal, but keep your
spiritual fervor, serving the Lord."
Romans 12:11

Zeal is deep, passionate devotion and
enthusiasm for God's work, driven by love for
him. It is the relentless energy and
determination to pursue a cause or purpose
with dedication.

Here are a few everyday examples:
-Begin your day with prayer and worship to
fuel your passion for God's work.
-Enthusiastically participating in ministry.

-Actively sharing the Gospel with joy
-Approaching your work or studies with a motivated and committed attitude.
-Encouraging others to participate in positive causes or initiatives you care about.

Simplicity

"But godliness with contentment is great gain.
For we brought nothing into the world, and
we can take nothing out of it. But if we have
food and clothing, we will be content with
that."
1 Timothy 6:6-8

Living with simplicity requires a content
heart, one free from greed or materialism,
fully anchored in God's will. It's about
avoiding unnecessary complications. Focusing
on what truly matters - faith, relationships,
health and letting go of excess stress and
worldly pressures. By embracing simplicity,
we can find greater joy and fulfillment in
todays fast paced and often chaotic world.

Here are a few everyday examples:

-Avoid overspending on material goods and
focus on acts of giving and gratitude.
-Practice gratitude for what you have.
- Avoid overcommitment
- Prioritize faith, prayer and inner peace

Encourage one another

"Therefore encourage one another and build
each other up."
1 Thessalonians 5:11

Encouragement is the act of uplifting and
motivating others, helping them grow in faith
and remain steadfast in God's promises.
It involves offering support, inspiration,
hope, reassurance and confidence to others
during challenging times with words, actions
and sometimes just presence. Encouragement
fosters love, unity and perseverance, helping
people stay motivated and faithful.

Here are a few everyday examples:
-Send a kind message or Scripture to someone
going through a tough time.

-Share your challenges and pray together.
-Commit to checking in regularly on each other's progress.
-Join or lead a small group to share testimonies and encourage each other spiritually.

Guard your heart

"Above all else, guard your heart, for
everything you do flows from it."
Proverbs 4:23

Guarding your heart means protecting your
inner thoughts, feelings, and desires from
anything that could lead you astray from
God's will. It's about keeping your heart pure,
focused on God's love and truth.
It is being careful about what influences
you—whether through the media you
consume, the people you surround yourself
with, or the thoughts you allow to grow in
your mind.

Here are a few everyday examples:
-Spend time in prayer each day, asking God
to protect your thoughts and feelings.
-Reflect on your emotions, making sure they
align with God's love and peace.
-Reflect on your feelings regularly, and if any
negative emotions like anger, jealousy, or
bitterness arise, bring them to God in prayer.
-Surround yourself with people who
encourage your spiritual growth and speak
positively into your life.

Justice

"Learn to do right; seek justice. Defend the
oppressed. Take up the cause of the fatherless;
plead the case of the widow."
Isaiah 1:17

Justice means standing up for what is right,
defending the oppressed, and treating
everyone fairly. It's about making sure others
are treated equally and with respect.

Here are a few everyday examples:
-Speak out when you see someone being
treated unfairly.

-Volunteer for organizations that fight for justice, like those that support the homeless or advocate for equality.
-Help create a fair and just environment in your community or workplace.

Gentleness

"Let your gentleness be evident to all. The Lord is near."
Philippians 4:5

Gentleness is the practice of being tender, patient, and calm. It's about responding with understanding and compassion, reflecting God's presence in your life. Handling situations and people with care, patience, and kindness. It is not a sign of weakness but strength.

Here are a few everyday examples:

- Correcting someone's mistake with understanding and grace.
- Holding back hurtful words.
- Being calm with someone who's struggling.
- Offering support instead of judgment.

Purity

"Blessed are the pure in heart, for they will see God."
Matthew 5:8

Purity of heart means being clean in thought, word, deed and free from corruption or immoral influences. It is about maintaining moral integrity and avoiding actions that compromise your values. Though it is not always easy, we need to pray for a clean heart and seek God's guidance daily.

Here are a few everyday examples:
-Avoiding gossip and negative talk.

-Guarding your thoughts and avoiding
harmful content.
-Avoid watching or consuming media that
promotes immorality or negativity.
-Dress and act modestly, honoring yourself
and others.
-Confess and pray regularly for a clean heart,
asking God to remove impurities.

Loyalty

"A friend loves at all times, and a brother is
born for a time of adversity."
Proverbs 17:17

Loyalty is unwavering faithfulness to God,
His Word, and His people, regardless of the
challenges. It means standing firm in
commitment, demonstrating trustworthiness
and devotion.

Here are a few everyday examples:

-Stand by your loved ones during difficult
times, offering support and encouragement.

-Stay committed to your faith by attending church, reading the Bible, and praying consistently.

-Be loyal to your workplace or team by doing your best, even when unacknowledged.

Responsibility

"Whatever you do, work at it with all your
heart, as working for the Lord, not for human
masters."
Colossians 3:23

Responsibility means diligently fulfilling the
tasks God has entrusted to you, whether big
or small. Being accountable for your actions,
duties, and commitments in life.

Here are few everyday examples:
-Meet deadlines and fulfill commitments with
diligence.
-Take responsibility for mistakes, apologize
sincerely, and learn from them.

-Prioritize family, work, and spiritual
obligations wisely.

Sacrifice

"Greater love has no one than this: to lay down one's life for one's friends."
John 15:13

Sacrifice is giving up personal desires, time, or resources in alignment with God's will or the benefit of others. Letting go of personal comfort or convenience to help or uplift someone else.

Here are a few everyday examples:
-Offer your time to serve others, even when it's inconvenient.
-Donate money, food, or resources to those in need, even if it means cutting back personally.

-Put aside personal ambitions to spend
quality time with family or friends in need.

Obedience

"If you love me, keep my commands."
John 14:15

Obedience is the act of willingly surrendering to God's commands and trusting His guidance, even when it's difficult. Following rules, instructions, or authority out of respect and discipline. Obedience brings blessings, peace and a deeper relationship with God. It gives you a sense of satisfaction.

Here are a few everyday examples:
-Read and meditate on God's Word, applying its teachings in your decisions.
-Respect workplace policies or leadership, even when it feels inconvenient.

-Teach children to respect authority and
follow instructions.
-Seek God's help to follow his plan, even if it
differs from your desires.

Watchfulness

"Be on your guard; stand firm in the faith; be
courageous; be strong."
1 Corinthians 16:13

Watchfulness means staying alert to spiritual
dangers. Being cautious, attentive, and ready
for potential challenges or changes.

Here are few everyday examples:
-Start your day with prayer, asking God for
wisdom to stay alert to sin.
-Be vigilant about negative influences in your
environment, such as harmful media or
relationships.

-Keep an eye out for opportunities to serve or help someone in need.
-Regularly reflect on your actions to ensure they align with God's will.

Long Suffering

"Be completely humble and gentle; be patient, bearing with one another in love."
Ephesians 4:2

Long-suffering is enduring pain, hardship, or mistreatment with patience and trust in God's plan. Demonstrating patience and endurance without resentment during prolonged trials or difficulties.

Here are few everyday examples:
-Respond to difficult people with patience and prayer instead of anger.

-Trust God's timing when waiting for answers
to prayers or life changes.
-Endure trials at work, family, or health by
focusing on God's promises.
-Support a loved one going through their own
trials, offering comfort and encouragement.